This copy of

MY HELP COMES FROM THE LORD

comes to

[redacted]

with love from

[redacted]

God BLESS YOU ALWAYS.

British Library Cataloguing-in-Publication Data. A catalogue record for this book is available from the British Library.
Published by Eagle, an imprint of Inter Publishing Service (IPS) Ltd, St Nicholas House, 14 The Mount, Guildford, Surrey GU2 5HN.

Typset by Eagle
Printed in Singapore
ISBN: 0 86347 260 5

MY HELP COMES FROM THE LORD

PILGRIM PSALMS

eagle

Guildford, Surrey

Let us go to the house of the Lord

I rejoiced with those who said to me,
    'Let us go to the house of the LORD.'
Our feet are standing
    in your gates, O Jerusalem.

Jerusalem is built like a city
    that is closely compacted together.
That is where the tribes go up,
    the tribes of the LORD
    according to the statute given to Israel.
There the thrones for judgment stand,
    the thrones of the house of David.

Pray for the peace of Jerusalem:
    'May those who love you be secure.
May there be peace within your walls
    and security within your citadels.'
For the sake of my brothers and friends,
    I will say, 'Peace be within you.'
For the sake of the house of the LORD our God,
    I will seek your prosperity.

Psalm 122:1–9

Jerusalem from the Hill of Evil Council,
Thomas Seddon

I lift up my eyes to you

I lift up my eyes to you,
to you whose throne is in heaven.
As the eyes of slaves look to the hand of their master,
as the eyes of a maid look to the hand of her mistress,
so our eyes look to the LORD our God,
till he shows us his mercy.

Psalm 123:1–2

A Prayer, Henry Le Jeune

If the Lord had not been on our side

If the LORD had not been on our side –
    let Israel say –
if the LORD had not been on our side
    when men attacked us,
when their anger flared against us,
    they would have swallowed us alive;
the flood would have engulfed us,
    the torrent would have swept over us,
the raging waters
    would have swept us away.
Psalm 124:1–5

The Mill Stream, Ernest Walbourne

Our help is in the name of the Lord

Praise be to the LORD,
  who has not let us be torn by their teeth.
We have escaped like a bird
  out of the fowler's snare;
the snare has been broken,
  and we have escaped.
Our help is in the name of the LORD,
  the Maker of heaven and earth.

Psalm 124:6–8

The Entangled Kite, Myles Birket Foster

The Lord surrounds his people

Those who trust in the LORD are like Mount Zion,
which cannot be shaken but endures forever.
As the mountains surround Jerusalem,
so the LORD surrounds his people
both now and for evermore.

The sceptre of the wicked will not remain
over the land alloted to the righteous,
for then the righteous might use
their hands to do evil.

Do good, O LORD, to those who are good,
to those who are upright in heart.
Psalm 125:1–4

Feeding the Chickens, Ernest Walbourn

The Lord has done great things for us

When the LORD brought back the captives to Zion,
we were like men who dreamed.
Our mouths were filled with laughter,
our tongues with songs of joy.
Then it was said among the nations,
'The LORD has done great things for them.'
The LORD has done great things for us,
and we are filled with joy.

Restore our fortunes, O LORD,
like streams in the Negev.
Those who sow in tears
will reap with songs of joy.
He who goes out weeping,
carrying seed to sow,
will return with songs of joy,
carrying sheaves with him.

Psalm 126:1–6

Harvest – Tying the Sheaves, Sir George Clausen

May the Lord bless you from Zion

Blessed are all who fear the LORD,
who walk in his ways.
You will eat the fruit of your labour;
blessings and prosperity will be yours.
Your wife will be like a fruitful vine
within your house;
your sons will be like olive shoots
round your table.
Thus is the man blessed
who fears the LORD.

May the LORD bless you from Zion
all the days of your life;
may you see the prosperity of Jerusalem,
and may you live to see your children's
children.

Peace be upon Israel.

Psalm 128:1–6

Picking Apples, Frederick Morgan

My soul waits for the Lord

Out of the depths I cry to you, O LORD;
O LORD, hear my voice.
Let your ears be attentive
to my cry for mercy.

If you, O LORD, kept a record of sins,
O LORD, who could stand?
But with you there is forgiveness;
therefore you are feared.

I wait for the LORD, my soul waits,
and in his word I put my hope.
My soul waits for the LORD
more than watchmen waiting for the morning,
more than watchmen waiting for the morning.

O Israel, put your hope in the LORD,
for with the LORD is unfailing love
and with him is full redemption.
He himself will redeem Israel
from all their sins.

Psalm 130:1–8

Day-Dreams on the Sea Shore, Edith Hume

I have stilled and quietened my soul

My heart is not proud, O LORD,
my eyes are not haughty;
I do not concern myself with great matters
or things too wonderful for me.
But I have stilled and quietened my soul;
like a weaned child with its mother,
like a weaned child is my soul within me.
Psalm 131:1–2

Precious Moments, Edwin Harris

Edwin Harris.

Let us go to his dwelling place

O Lord, remember David
    and all the hardships he endured.

He swore an oath to the Lord
    and made a vow to the Mighty One of Jacob:
'I will not enter my house
    or go to my bed –
I will allow no sleep to my eyes,
    no slumber to my eyelids,
till I find a place for the Lord,
    a dwelling for the Mighty One of Jacob.'. . .

'Let us go to his dwelling place;
    let us worship at his footstool –
arise, O Lord, and come to your resting place,
    you and the ark of your might.
May your priests be clothed with righteousness;
    may your saints sing for joy.'

Psalm 132:1–9

In Church, George Goodwin Kilburne

The Lord has chosen Zion

The LORD swore an oath to David,
    a sure oath that he will not revoke:
'One of your own descendants
    I will place on your throne –
if your sons keep my covenant
    and the statutes I teach them,
then their sons shall sit on your throne for ever
    and ever.

For the LORD has chosen Zion,
    he has desired it for his dwelling:
'This is my resting place for ever and ever;
    here I will sit enthroned, for I have desired it.
I will bless her with abundant provisions;
    her poor will I satisfy with food.
I will clothe her priests with salvation,
    and her saints shall ever sing for joy.

Here I will make a horn grow for David
    and set up a lamp for my anointed one.
I will clothe his enemies with shame,
    but the crown on his head shall be
        resplendent.'

Psalm 132:11–18

Lunchtime Preparations, William Kay Blacklock

Praise the Lord

Praise the LORD, all you servants of the LORD
who minister by night in the house of the LORD.
Lift up your hands in the sanctuary
and praise the LORD.

May the LORD, the Maker of heaven and earth,
bless you from Zion.

Psalm 134:1–3

The Village Choir, Thomas Webster

My help comes from the Lord

I lift up my eyes to the hills –
where does my help come from?
My help comes from the LORD,
the Maker of heaven and earth.

He will not let your foot slip –
he who watches over you will not slumber;
indeed, he who watches over Israel
will neither slumber nor sleep.

The LORD watches over you –
the LORD is your shade at your right hand;
the sun will not harm you by day,
nor the moon by night.

The LORD will keep you from all harm –
he will watch over your life;
the LORD will watch over your coming and going
both now and for evermore.

Psalm 121:1–8

Gathering Poppies, Ernest Walbourne

Unless the Lord builds the house

Unless the LORD builds the house,
  its builders labour in vain.
Unless the LORD watches over the city,
  the watchmen stand guard in vain.
In vain you rise early
  and stay up late,
toiling for food to eat –
  for he grants sleep to those he loves.

Sons are a heritage from the LORD,
  children a reward from him.
Like arrows in the hands of a warrior
  are sons born in one's youth.
Blessed is the man
  whose quiver is full of them.
They will not be put to shame
  when they contend with their enemies in the gate.

Psalm 127:1–5

At West Tarring, Helen Allingham

Picture Credits

Eagle Publishing is grateful to the The Fine Art Picture Library who hold copyright for all the illustrations, unless otherwise indicated, for their kind permission to reproduce the paintings selected to complement the text.

cover *The Mill Stream,* Ernest Walbourne (1897-1927?).
1 *Jerusalem from the Hill of Evil Council,* Thomas Seddon (1821-1856), copyright Tate Gallery.
2 *A Prayer,* Henry Le Jeune (1819-1904).
3 *The Mill Stream,* Ernest Walbourne (1897-1927?).
4 *The Entangled Kite,* Myles Birket Foster (1825-1899).
5 *Feeding the Chickens,* Ernest Walbourne (1897-1927?).
6 *Harvest – Tying the Sheaves*, Sir George Caulsen (1852-1944), courtesy Richard Green Gallery.
7 *Picking Apples,* Frederick Morgan (1856-1927), courtesy John Nott Gallery.
8 *Day-Dreams on the Sea Shore,* Edith Hume (1862-1992), courtesy Polak Gallery.
9 *Precious Moments,* Edwin Harris (1855-1906).
10 *In Church,* George Goodwin Kilburne (1839-1924), courtesy of Sotheby's Bond Street.
11 *Lunchtime Preparations,* William Kay Blacklock, (d.1924), courtesy Mensing Gallery.
12 *The Village Choir*, Thomas Webster (1800-1886), copyright Bridgeman Art Library and V&A.
13 *Gathering Poppies*, Ernest Walbourne (1897-1927?), courtesy Caelt Gallery.
14 *At West Tarring*, Helen Allingham (1848-1926), copyright Eagle.